EMERALD BUSINESS GUIDES

EMERALD BUSINESS
Business Start up and Future Planning

Gordon Clarke

www.emeraldpublishing.co.uk

Emerald Publishing
Brighton BN2 4EG

© Straightforward Publishing 2007

ISBN 1847160 034 4
ISBN 13: 978184716 034 8

Printed by Biddles Ltd Kings Lynn Norfolk

Cover design by Bookworks Islington

Whilst every effort has been made to ensure that the information
contained within this book is correct at the time of going to
press, the author and publisher can take no responsibility for the
errors or omissions contained within.

Contents

1

Initial Thoughts-Thinking Through Ideas and Plans

It is very important, right at the outset, to have a clear idea of why exactly you want to go into business. Many people have vague ideas of why they want to start a business. Quite often, no experience at all is involved, just a basic desire to either achieve independence, make money, conquer the world or whatever. Achieving independence and making money are laudable goals, conquering the world is not really a goal.

Most often, people will develop businesses from a hobby or a part time activity that expands with time and turns into a business. However, if this is the case, it must be clear that sufficient profit can be generated to earn a living and provide for further expansion.

Skills required to run a business

Anyone who wishes to start up and run their own business needs to understand that it is very different to working in a nine-to-five job. Working for an employer means that you have the security of an income, pension, defined working hours, protection through legislation and fixed holidays. Not so when you run your own business. Although you have protection through legislation, you cease to be an employee in the traditional sense and you work for yourself. This entails long hours, uncertain rewards and uncertain outcomes. In short you will need to possess qualities that will enable you to run a business. These qualities are:

- Self-discipline and the ability to work hard
- Motivation and enthusiasm
- The ability to withstand pressure
- The ability to make decisions
- The ability to relate to people

When you run a business you no longer work for someone else, with that person taking all the strain but you are now on your own and have to provide the direction for your business and any other people involved in it.

The nature of your business

Obviously, if you have taken the decision to start your own business, you should have some idea of what it is that you want to do. Maybe you don't, but have picked up this book to give you some ideas.

Most people will be entering the market place with a product that is in competition with others. Quite often, the market place is crowded. It is very important if this is the case to understand what your unique selling point (USP) is and what competitive advantage you are offering. Are you offering lower prices, a better standard of service or faster response if breakdowns occur. The advantages that you can offer will depend on your business and the type of service. However, it is important to know that, if you are entering into competition with others, then the only way you can gain any market share is by having an advantage that will appeal to customers and also a clear idea of how you are going to launch your business, where you are going to launch it and who your target group is going to be. These areas will be thoroughly explored as we work through this book.

The ways of starting a business

There are several ways to start a business. You can start it from nothing, you can buy into a franchise or buy an existing business.

Starting from nothing

This is possibly the most difficult and certainly the riskiest way of starting a business. You will need to have researched the market thoroughly, know what you are doing, where you are going, have formulated a plan and have finance in place. Money is always tight in the early days and it is vitally important that you don't waste money or take bad advice. A fool and his or her money are easily parted.

The key to initial start ups is to keep things small to start with. Spending money on unnecessary things means less profits and less chance of survival. Only start a business in an area where you have sound knowledge. If you don't you will spend a lot of expensive time learning from your mistakes.

Franchises

Franchises are businesses that have already been tried and tested in the market place. The concept has been proven although this doesn't guarantee success for you as an owner/franchisee. It is true to say that there are very many dubious franchise out there which are based on ideas and theories but are not proven to be a success. The pages of Daltons weekly are littered with them and the only person who gets rich is the person who has put the franchise idea together. Sure for £10,000 you can get a smart new uniform, a van and a 'round' cleaning wheelie bins or whatever the idea is, but will you make money?

With good franchises, support will be offered as the franchisor knows that if you fail he will not make money. Many of the big companies, such as Mail Boxes Etc and Kall-Kwik printing have operated successfully for years. As with many businesses there is an element of risk but the number of business failures is less with franchises than with new business start ups. We will look at franchising in greater depth later on in the book.

Purchasing an existing business

Having purchased an existing business myself, I can point out a number of pitfalls that can prove to be disastrous. One of the first problems is trying to establish a value for the business. There is a definite need to make sure that you know why the business is for sale and a very definite need to get the accounts independently audited. We will look at the mechanics of buying an existing business later on.

2

Taking Stock of Legislation when Starting a Business

Businesses vary in nature and some legislation will be pertinent to a specific business whilst not specific to others. It is vitally important that you have a thorough knowledge of legislation before you commence a business. For example, if you are planning to open a restaurant then the law that you have to comply with, mainly health and safety based, will be different to starting a graphic design company.

However, there are laws which all business will have to comply with and these are outlined below. These laws are concerned mainly with starting a business, the different types of company that you can start, naming your business, copyright, VAT and so on.

The different types of company

Most business will take one of three forms:

- Sole trader
- Partnership
- Limited company

Obviously, before progressing a business you will need to know the nature of each type of business, the reasons why you should adopt a specific type of business and the legal ramifications. This will perhaps involve a consultation with an accountant or lawyer in order to make sure that you are clear.

Operating as a sole trader

Setting up as a sole trader is without doubt one of the simplest ways to start up in business. There are very few formalities other than informing the Inland Revenue that you are about to become self employed, for the purposes of tax and National Insurance contributions. You are in sole charge and any profits from the enterprise are yours. However, so are any debts and if you fail you will lose everything, or at least anything which has a value and can cover losses. You will have a responsibility to maintain books of accounts for tax and VAT purposes although you do not, as a limited company does, have to make them available.

Starting a partnership

A word of warning about entering into partnerships. Make sure that both you and you prospective partner can operate together and trust each other. The business world has been littered with failed partnerships. Try, if at all possible, to keep business and friendship at arms length. They never mix well.

Other than that, a partnership is much the same as sole trading with all the partners sharing responsibility for managing the business. The same applies to any debts and liabilities that occur within the business, they are shared.

It is very important to formalise the partnership at the outset. This can be achieved through a deed of partnership, signed by all parties. This gives it a clear framework and prevents the moving of goalposts down the line. Everybody involved knows where they stand in terms of their role in the company and also future profit sharing. Never start life as a partnership on the basis of promises or trust. This usually goes wrong. Again, you will want to obtain initial advice from a solicitor or an accountant. In addition, Companies House will provide advice free of charge.

Setting up a limited company

There are four main types of limited company:

- A private company which is limited by shares-the members liability is limited to the amount unpaid on shares they hold
- A private company which is limited by guarantee-members liability is limited to the amount they have agreed to contribute to the company's assets if it is wound up
- A private unlimited company-there is no limit to the members liability
- A Public limited company (PLC)-the company's shares can be offered for sale to the general public and the members liability is limited to the amount unpaid on shares held by them.

For a new business starting up, a private company limited by shares is the most common type of trading vehicle. It is possible to buy a ready made company or equally possible to form a company yourself using your own chosen name. The start point for this is contacting Companies House either through their website (see useful addresses at end of book) or phoning them on 029 2038 0801.

After setting up a limited company, owners have to comply with strict accounting requirements and have to lodge accounts annually with Companies House. Over the years this procedure has tightened up because of previous abuse of the whole system. It is usually necessary to ensure that you have an accountant to prepare accounts and also VAT if this is involved.

Business names

If you decide to use a name other than your own as your business name you will need to comply with the requirements of the Business Names Act 1985. This Act applies to all businesses, whether sole trader, partnerships or companies. It applies to:

- A company which trades under a name which is not its corporate name
- A partnership which does not trade under the name of all the partners
- An individual who trades under a name which is not his or her name

It is possible to use virtually any name you want to trade under with the following exceptions, which will require permission from the Secretary of State:

- British
- International
- United Kingdom
- European
- National

These words imply national or international pre-eminence. In the same way it is not possible to use names which imply business pre-eminence or representative status, such as:

- Association
- Council
- Institution
- Authority
- Federation
- Society
- Board
- Institute

Under the Act, there are strict requirements in relation to disclosure of the owners of a business which is using a trading name. It is necessary to disclose the corporate name or the name of each partner or the individual persons name and an address for each individual where documents can be served. This information has to be shown in all the places where you carry on business, on all stationary, invoices and receipts and business orders.

Although there is no longer any legal requirement to register a trading name, if you copy another businesses name or trademark it could lead to legal action against you. Although, when registering a limited company, a check will be carried out for identical names, this same check will not be carried out for sole traders or partnerships. It will be necessary to use the services of Business names Registration plc (BNR) which has access to databases covering several million business names, and limited company names and other registered trademarks. For a small fee BNR will check your business name and add it to their register.

Protecting ideas (intellectual property)

In order to protect your ideas being exploited by others, it is necessary to have a clear understanding of copyright and patent laws. Business names and logos can be protected by registering them as trademarks.

A patent will protect an invention or something that is unique. Applying for a patent is complex and usually expensive but it is difficult to succeed without the help of the experts. If you want to go ahead and make your own application in order to avoid hefty costs then you can contact the patent office or its website (address at the back of book). They will issue clear guidance on the process.

Copyright
One of the most misunderstood areas and the one that leads to the most trouble between people is that of

copyright. Copyright is the creator's legal rights over his or her work, for example:

- Artwork
- Writing
- Graphic design
- Computer programmes

The list is long and it is important to understand how this works. Unlike patents, which need to be registered, copyright happens automatically. For example, as you create, the copyright is also being created and it will be necessary to indicate somewhere that copyright belongs to the creator (named creator). In a book for example this will be at the beginning of the book on the copyright page.

Trademarks

Once you have chosen a name for your business and products you can protect all of them by applying for a trademark from the Trademarks Registry at the Patent Office.

Dealing with the Inland Revenue

If the type of business that you have started is a sole trader or a partnership then this will come under the Inland Revenue Self-Assessment Scheme for payment of income tax and National Insurance Contributions. If you are a limited company then this will also be liable for Corporation Tax. As an employee of a limited company you will be liable for income tax and national insurance in the same way as any other employee.

National Insurance

There are three types of NI contributions:

- Class one-applies to all employed people and is paid by both the employer and employee
- Class two- paid at a flat rate by all self-employed people whether they are sole traders or partners
- Class three-payable by the self employed as a percentage of profits between a minimum and maximum level.

Tax return

About the safest way to ensure that you deal with this return, the Self-Assessment return, is to get an accountant to do it for you. Their fees are usually offset by the tax saving s that can be made.

VAT

Someone or some entity has to collect VAT on behalf of the government. Overseeing the whole operation is the Customs and Excise and acting as unpaid tax collectors are the legion of small and large businesses.

Whatever form of business that has been chosen, it will be necessary to consider the implications of whether or not you want to register for VAT. VAT is a tax that businesses charge when they supply their goods and services within the UK. It is also charged on some imports and exports from EU member states.

At present there are three VAT rates:

- 17.5% - standard rate charged on most goods and services
- 5% - reduced rate charged on domestic fuel and power and by charities
- 0% - this is where no VAT is charged.

If the turnover of a business exceeds a limit set down by HM Customs and Excise (website and address at back of book), then the owner becomes a taxable person and you must register for VAT. Following registration then it will be necessary to fill in a VAT return every three months and send it off. If you are expecting a refund and are not voluntarily registered it is possible to do monthly returns. The amount charged others for VAT is set off against what you have charged and the difference is either paid or repaid to you.

Non-standard VAT returns

If your accounting system is not based on calendar months, because of the particular nature of your business, you can apply for VAT return dates that fit with your business.

Annual returns

If you have been registered for VAT for at least 12 months and your business has a taxable turnover below a set threshold you can apply to make annual VAT returns. Under this scheme, you account for VAT by making nine monthly payments based on an estimate of the annual VAT that will be due to you. You then send in your annual return with a final balance payment two months after the end of the year.

Cash accounting scheme

This is available to businesses with taxable turnover below the set level. It allows for the accounting of VAT on the basis of payments received and made rather than on invoices that are issued and received. This can be of benefit to some business which allow long periods of credit or have high levels of bad debts.

A word of warning. Many people spend ages sifting through mounds of receipts and try to complete their own VAT return in order to save on accountants fees. Beware of this as Customs and Excise carry out periodic checks on business and invariably they unearth mistakes. They also require every receipt/ invoice and other financial record relating to the period in question.

In short, use an accountant to prepare your VAT return and only register for VAT if you really have to!

3

Setting out Clear Objectives for your Business and Defining a Business Strategy

In this chapter we will look at the process of setting objectives for a business, i.e. what are your aims and goals. We will also look at the development of a business strategy.

It is absolutely essential to have a crystal clear idea of what the main objectives for your business are. Business objectives relate to a business as a whole and to what you want to achieve in the long and short term.

Short term objectives will relate to what you want to achieve on an annual basis, over a period of twelve months. Long term objectives relate to a period (usually) of five years.

It has become commonplace now to set up a criteria against which you can measure the effectiveness of your business objectives. This is known as 'SMART' criteria. Within SMART all the objectives that you set for your business must be:

- Specific

- Measurable
- Agreed
- Realistic
- Timed

The above are self explanatory and enable a business owner to set clear objectives which can be re-evaluated over time. SMART objectives should be set against a clear MISSION Statement.

Mission statements

The best way to quantify business statements is through a mission statement. The mission statement is really a vision statement which details the whole point of your business. There are four key components of a mission statement which must be succinct and clear:

- The role or contribution that a business makes-what exactly are you in business for?
- A definition of the business-this should be given in terms of the benefits you provide or the needs that you satisfy. It should not define what you do or what you make.
- An outline of your distinctive competencies-the factors that differentiate your business from the competition. These are the skills and capabilities that are offered by you as opposed to other business in the same field
- The indications for the future-what the business will do in the future, what it can realistically achieve.

A clear and coherent mission statement is written in two parts. In the first part you will outline the industry that you are in and the products that you offer. The second part comprises the business strategies that you will follow to achieve success. A few examples might be:

- We will provide a first class service to all customers
- We will achieve high productivity levels through sound planning, organisation and teamwork
- We will generate sufficient profits to ensure ongoing investment in the business
- We will earn high employee loyalty and motivation by respecting their capabilities and their motivation and providing training opportunities
- We will gain recognition in the market for being a highly professional, ethical, quality assured business.

Obviously, the above needs to be fleshed out and thought through but it is the basis upon which the operations of your business will be founded and on which the SMART objectives will integrate in order to ensure that the business moves forward and achieves its goals.

Mission statements need to be re-evaluated on a regular basis as there is always the ever present danger that it will become just a form of words that sounds good but has no bearing in reality.

Taking SMART objectives and Mission Statements further, basic marketing objectives should mesh with both. We will be looking at marketing later in the book.

Defining your business strategy

As the owner of your business, or one of the owners, you will be responsible for defining business strategy. Strategic management, essentially, has three components:

- Analysis-where are you now and where do you want to be?
- Choice-what options are available to you?
- Implementation-implement your strategy based on the analysis and options.

Strategic analysis

There are two distinct areas of any business that require analysis:

- The environment
- The resources of the business

PESTE analysis

There are a number of factors in the environment that can have an impact on your business. The PESTE analysis enables you to focus on these. PESTE stands for:

- P = political
- E = Economic

- S = Social
- T = Technological
- E = Environment

Political

When examining the effect of political forces on a business we are really referring to legislation which has a direct impact on business, such as health and safety legislation and employment law. It is necessary to comply with all legislation and to be seen to be doing so.

Economic

Economic forces will include all the variables that may have an effect of the profitability and sustainability of your business. These can include, inflation, interest rates and, if you trade abroad, interest rates. Changes in the budget will also, invariably, have an effect on you.

Social

Social forces can be complex and include demographic changes that will affect your business. For example, if you sell shoes, the fact that there is a falling birth rate in a particular part of the country may affect demand, will affect demand, for the type and size of shoes needed over the longer term.

Technological

The rapid changes in information technology and relevance to all businesses must be taken into account when devising future strategy.

Environmental

The impact of business on the environment must be evaluated and taken into account when formulating any business strategy.

Auditing resources

Having considered the business environment through PESTE, we should now look at auditing the resources of the business. If the business is new then an analysis of what resources might be required to achieve your aims will be necessary. There are three main headings under which your resources will fall:

- Physical resources
- Human resources
- Financial resources

Physical resources

Physical resources include plant, machines, tool, vehicles and so on. An audit of these resources whether existing or needed in the future will include longevity, cost of future replacement and also maintenance.

Human resources

This will be an assessment of staff needed in the future, if you are a new business, or existing staff if you are established. An audit of human resources should take into account staff development, which will be based on the future skills requirements of staff allied to your own strategy for the business. We will look at staff later in the book.

Financial resources

This area, like the other two, is of vital importance. Without financial stability the business will not survive. An audit of financial resources will include all the sources of finance that you have. This audit will also include an analysis of debtors and creditors. The end result should be a clear determination of current and future viability and, if problems are identified, the rectification of these problems.

Evaluation of future options

The next step in the process, after completing the analysis of your business, is the evaluation of all the different options that have been thrown up. This evaluation has to be alongside the business goals and objectives previously set.

Generally, when assessing options, there will be four available:

- Consider withdrawing from the market completely
- Consolidate the existing position within the market
- Increase market penetration
- Introduce new products or services.

The above will clearly emerge following your analysis of the business.

Withdrawing from the market can mean liquidation or sale of the business. Consolidation is usually an internal process where the business may concentrate on overall efficiency. Increased market penetration essentially means expanding into new markets for existing products and services. Introduction of new products and services can mean adapting the existing technology or products to suit new markets.

Strategic implementation

There are two aspects of implementation that you need to consider. One is planning carefully the other is the actual implementation. There are three key areas into which you can break down the implementation process:

- Planning and allocation of resources
- The structure of the business
- Management of the people and the systems in the business.

Planning and allocation of resources

The resources of a business, as we have seen, are physical, human and financial. For a new business it should be fairly easy to plan what resources are needed and then allocate them. However, this is more complex for a growing business.

The planning of physical and human resources will be easier than the planning of financial resources. We will look at financial forecasting later on in the book.

The structure of a business

Again, if the business is new the structure is likely to be less complicated than a growing business. Initially, in a new business, management can be hands on. In a growing business management will need to be delegated. This will involve a clear idea of the direction of the business, of the integration of different tasks. It is, however, very important that the owner of the business has complete financial control.

Management of people and systems in a business

If it is necessary to employ staff in your business then it is very important indeed that you have staff management strategies in place. When considering management planning in this area there are a number of considerations:

- What do you want from your staff-what is their function?
- How do you want them to perform-to achieve the task in hand?
- When do you want them to perform?
- What will be the salary structure and overall cost?
- What training will be provided to enable them to perform and to achieve greater ob satisfaction?

The question of staff management and motivation, and the meshing of all the tasks to produce satisfactory outcomes is one of the most difficult areas of business management next to financial management.

Business control systems

Integral to all businesses is the need for a management information system. This will enable you to control your business effectively. The main areas where you will need an information system are:

- Financial performance-the ability to analyse how the company is doing and where it is going in the future
- An ongoing analysis of the marketplace
- A sales and distribution analysis
- A Physical resource analysis
- Human resource analysis.

The above are not exhaustive but are the key indicators from which you can draw information to enable you to manage the business in the present and the future. We will look at management systems later in the book.

Strategic threats

In business, there are ever present threats to the viability of your business, to your market share. These can be from new entrants into the market place, i.e. new companies, the threat of other products (substitute products), this could be an imitation of your product but cheaper, the power of suppliers and buyers, effectively the ability to create monopolies and control prices and competitive rivalry from other companies.. These factors need to be analysed on a regular basis because if they aren't then you will find yourself at a sudden disadvantage.

4

The Support Network For New Businesses

When starting your own business, it is important to know that there is a strong support network out there which will provide assistance in various areas of business activity. The support available is both financial and non-financial. In this chapter we will be looking at the non-financial support network.

In the UK, business slinks exist to provide advice and assistance to businesses. This is usually free although there may be a small fee for certain services. The usual help centres around business administration, business planning, marketing, fund raising and legislation.

Business Links also provide other help such as business information based on research, a Personal Business Advisor and also access to seminars and conferences which provide networking opportunities with other businesses. Other organisations providing support are Enterprise Agencies providing advice, counselling, training and other practical assistance to businesses.

British Chambers of Commerce

To be a member of the BCC is quite expensive, proportionate to the size of a business. However, the services offered are numerous and the advantages are clear. The BCC offers training and advice and also promotes networking opportunities to members. They also offer advice and assistance on exporting and can arrange attendance at trade fairs across the globe.

The Federation of Small Businesses

The FSB is the largest campaign group working on behalf of small businesses and also self-employed people. Membership fees are based on a sliding scale depending on numbers of employees. Free services such as telephone helplines and expert advice, legal assistance and financial advice are available.

The FSB also provides legal and professional insurance of up to £1m to protect businesses against Inland Revenue investigations, VAT tribunals and appeals, industrial tribunal costs, employment disputes and other audit related activities.

The FSB will help in defending against prosecution in connection with Health and Safety at work issues, Consumer Protection issues, Food safety, Data protection, damage to property and personal injury.

Other organisations which provide help and assistance include:

- Shell *Live*WIRE which is a UK wide organisation that assists young business people, or potential business people wishing to start or develop their business

- The Outreach Programme-again acting as a gateway for young people who require advice and support
- The Forum of Private Business (FPB). This is a campaigning business support organisation offering help and advice
- Lawyers for your Business-lawyers participating in this scheme offer a number of services such as a free consultation with a solicitor and a free diagnosis from that solicitor.

5
Products/Markets/Pricing

The area of marketing is, without doubt, one of the most important areas of a business and the one which is usually neglected. Research and analysis of your potential market, whatever you are making or offering, is absolutely crucial to the success of your business.

Without customers to buy your products you cannot survive. With any marketing strategy, there are a number of questions that need to be answered at the outset:

- Who are the potential customers?
- What do they buy and why do they buy it?
- When do they buy and where do they buy?

The above questions are not exhaustive but are the key questions when carrying out initial research. Also important is the nature of the customer, how old, occupation, standard of education and income and family position, i.e. married, single, children and also their location. All these are important factors and research should help to shape your business plan.

Segmenting the market place

There are a number of different ways to segment customers and markets. There is no one perfect method.

Geographic segmentation

This is a simple form of segmentation and is relatively unsophisticated, consisting of dividing your market on the basis of geographical location of potential customers This is fine if all sales are made within one particular market. For example, if you are selling in the UK then you can segment customers by region.

Demographic segmentation

Demographic segmentation is a more sophisticated way of segmenting customers as it involves identifying potential customers according to specific variables such as age, sex, family size, income or lifestyle.

There are two main methods used to provide the different socio-economic groupings, the first classifies occupation and social class groups the second, known as ACORN (A Classification of residential Neighbourhoods) classifies types of neighbourhoods.

Occupation and social class

Here groups are segmented into 6 classes, A to E. Each one denotes a social class type as follows:

A = Higher managerial
B = Intermediate management
C1= Supervisor/ lower management
C2= Skilled manual
D = Semi-skilled/unskilled
E = Lowest level of subsistence

However, when making assumptions about social classes, care and skill is required as many assumptions such as disposable income may not be accurate.

ACORN

This method analyses people, or households, on the basis of the type of property. The information is derived from the census, undertaken every ten years with the next one due in 2011. This system is based on the assumption that consumer lifestyles and behaviour are closely related to neighbourhood types. Again, an alphabetical system is used, A to K, as follows:

A = Modern family housing for manual workers
B = Modern family housing for higher incomes
C = Older housing of intermediate status
D = Poor quality older terraced housing
E = Rural areas
F = Urban local authority housing
G = Housing with most overcrowding
H = Low income areas with migrants
I = Students and high status non-family areas
J = Transitional high status suburbia
K = Areas of elderly people

Product segmentation

This is a simple form of segmentation which is used to identify people who would buy, or potentially buy a particular product.

Benefit and lifestyle segmentation

This takes demographic segmentation one step further by linking the lifestyle of consumers to their decision to buy a particular product. The next step is to differentiate their product, either on quality or other claimed advantages. As we all know, quite often one product is the same as another. However, the manufacturer will differentiate his or her product by branding and association. Different groups will respond to different messages, such as the ability of a toothpaste to prevent tooth decay and to whiten the teeth and so on.

Competitive advantage

This is critical to all marketing. Businesses must differentiate their products from each other in order to gain market share. Competitive advantage can consist of either lower product prices or a better service than competitors. It is crucial that you understand your competitors if you are to obtain a competitive advantage. It is very important that you have as much information about your competitors as possible. You need to:

- Establish exactly who your competitors are
- Identify their marketing objectives
- Analyse their marketing strategies.

You should also look at whether they have any strengths and weaknesses. You can analyse their strengths and weaknesses, and also your own, by carrying out a SWOT analysis. SWOT is the acronym for Strengths, Weaknesses, Opportunities and Threats. A SWOT analysis is compiled using a grid to enable you to consider how you will match your strengths to your opportunities and how you can overcome your weaknesses and threats. Strengths and opportunities are listed in the left hand column and weaknesses and threats are listed in the right column.

Strengths	Weaknesses
Something that you are doing well or are good at. It could be a skill, competence or competitive advantage that you have over your business rivals.	Something that, by comparison to your rivals, you do poorly. This is a position that puts you at a disadvantage.
Opportunities	Threats
Look for realistic growth opportunities in the business	This is a factor that could lead to problems within your business and subsequent decline.

Unique selling points (USP)

This is a crucial element in defining the competitive advantage of your business. Identifying your Unique Selling Points will help you define what it is that makes you different from your competitors. You can use USP's in your marketing. There are a number of questions that need to be asked when identifying USP's:

- Will the customer perceive this as an advantage?

- Is it very different from what my competitors are offering?
- Will customers receive some benefit from the USP?
- Will the USP motivate customers to make a purchase?

Obviously, an advantage (or perceived advantage) must offer and give benefits over and above your competitor's products.

Within all markets there are a number of factors that will be critical to your success. Examples of critical success factors will be delivery time, speed of service, quality of the product and competitive pricing. Critical success factors will vary from industry to industry and market to market. There is no clear formula as to what will be important and crucial to you. It is vital that you identify your own critical success factors.

6

Location and Premises-Making the Right Choice

Location of your business

To be within easy reach of your customers may be vital or it may be totally unimportant. If you have a retail business, location is a major consideration. If you are in mail order, you can operate from anywhere in the country so far as your customers are concerned. If you are a wholesaler, do you require a showroom? If you are operating a factory, do you anticipate the requirement for a factory shop? is it simply a question of being conveniently located for your customers or are you relying on passing trade? It is vital that, in assessing the right location, you first clearly define the extent to which you need to make yourself accessible to your customers.

In an ideal world, you should be looking to acquire the right accommodation for your scale of operation today and for your expansion plans this year, next year and some years in the future. This applies whether you are looking for a shop, an office, a workshop or a factory unit. Before you start looking for new premises, work out carefully just what it is you need now.

The important questions to consider are:

- How many square feet of offices/storage space/workshop/showroom?

- How many square feet of employees facilities?

- How much car parking space?

- How much outside storage for deliveries, storage and packing?

If you are uncertain as to what precisely you need, or you feel that the shape of your business is going to alter substantially and in the short term, do not commit yourself to a hefty purchase, or even as much as a five year lease. Go instead for a temporary solution, while you determine what your long-term requirements are likely to be.

Never enter into a lengthy commitment unless you feel that the premises are likely to suit you in the long term. Whether you are buying a freehold or acquiring a lease, take independent professional advice on the value. Hire a surveyor who will tell you whether the asking price or rent is fair. Whatever your business, the cost of your premises is going to represent a major overhead. If you get it wrong, you will go out of business.

It is essential to establish that not only can the property be used for the purpose for which we want it, but also that the planning consent will cover any future business development.

Working from home

Particularly if you are starting a new business, the idea of working from home is attractive. It enables you to keep your overheads to a minimum, allows you to work the long hours necessary in the establishment of a business, and leaves your options open-if the business does not work out, you are not committed to an industrial property. It needs to be recognized, however, that working from home can cause considerable problems.

Strictly speaking, if you plan to run a business from home, almost certainly you will need approval or permission either from someone or some authority. There are two kinds of restrictions which may affect your ability to run your business from home. The first is a series of contractual relationships which you may have already entered into, such as a tenancy or lease. The second is that imposed by local authorities-planning, highways, health and safety.

Planning permission

If you want to make a significant alteration to your house in order to accommodate your business, you will need planning permission or building regulations approval. This includes building an extension, loft conversion, in fact almost anything except extremely simple alterations

Change of use

Local authorities state that consent has to be sought for any change of use. The interpretation of change of use is difficult but what you have to decide is whether what you wish to do constitutes a genuine material change of use of the building.

You should make sure that you have insurance to cover your business activity within your home. If you have an accident which occurs as a direct result of your business then your insurance will not cover it.

Health and Safety at work

Whatever your position in relationship to your premises, i.e., leasehold or freehold, under the terms of the Health and Safety at Work Act You have certain obligations to protect yourself, your staff, your customers and your suppliers. Health and Safety Legislation is very important and attention should be paid to it.

Inspectors

There are two types of inspector-local authority inspectors and fire authority inspectors. Local Authority inspectors are concerned with premises where the main activities are:

- The sale or storage of goods for retail or wholesale distribution.

- Office activities

- Catering Services

- Provision of residential accommodation

- Consumer services provided in shop premises

- Dry Cleaning in coin operated units in launderettes

- The keeping of wild animals for exhibition to the public

- Fire Authority inspectors

The fire authority requires that a place of work should have a fire certificate, and in order for your business to get a fire certificate, the premises need to be inspected. The fire authority will wish to see that there is adequate provision for a means of escape in case of fire, and the necessary amount of equipment. The Fire inspectors will advise you these facilities are inadequate, tell you how they can be put right and then re-inspect the premises when you have carried out the necessary work.

Employing People

At first you may be able to run your business by yourself or with help from your family. But if not, as your business expands, you may need to employ people. Before doing this, some businesses may consider it worthwhile subcontracting work. This may be more cost effective in ironing out short term trading highs and lows. However, if you do need to take on employees, then you must do certain things.

What are my responsibilities as an employer?

You must give every employee a written statement of terms of employment. At the time of publication, by law, all employees working 16 or more hours a week must be given a written statement of terms after they have worked 13 weeks in the job.

This statement must include the following:
- name of employer

- name of employee, job title and description

- hours of work

- pay details, including how often the employee is paid
- holidays

- grievance procedures

- sickness and injury procedures

- pension schemes

- length of notice needed to end employment

- disciplinary rules, including dress and behaviour

National Insurance Contributions

If you employ anybody, either full time or part time, you must take tax and national insurance contributions (NIC's) from their wages, and you must also pay the employers share of the NIC's, always consult your local contributions agency office. There are different tax and National Insurance Rules depending on your circumstances.

Discrimination and the law

It is against the law for an employer or a would-be employer to advertise a job that in any way discriminates against race or sex. After taking on an employee, the anti discrimination laws still apply to all other parts of the employees job, including wages and holidays.

Health and safety

Make sure you are in line with the health and safety regulations which lay down minimum standards for fire precautions and other safety issues. Contact your local health and safety executive for advice and information which will help you to set up and maintain safe and legal working conditions for employees.

Trade Unions

Make sure that you know about the various laws which safeguard your employees rights to choose whether to join a trade union.

Tax and National Insurance-more details

Once you regularly employ people, you are responsible for deducting their income tax and National Insurance Contributions, and paying your own employers NI contributions. When you take on someone, you need to tell your local tax office. You will be sent documents which will show you how much you need to take out of each employees wages, and where to send the money. You must record each employees earnings and tax and

51

National Insurance Contributions, and tell your local tax office about these amounts each year.

In the case of national Insurance, The contributions for your employees will be in two parts. You must pay one part and your employee will pay the other. These contributions depend on how much you pay your employee. The Inland Revenue will collect them at the same time as they collect any tax. Your local contributions agency office will be able to give you more advice on National Insurance.

Your personal insurance depends on your circumstances. If you are a company director, you will be treated in a similar way to your employees. You will be classed as an employee of your company and will pay contributions in the same way as your employees. But, there is no special way to assess directors National Insurance. You should contact the Contributions Agency Office for advice on this matter. If you are a sole trader, or partner, your contributions will be charged at the same rate each week. You must pay them every month by direct debit or every three months when you receive a bill. You may also have to pay an extra contribution for any profits your company makes. This is assessed and collected along with Income tax. You should tell the contribution's agency office as soon as you become self- employed.

The law and you as an employer

Having considered some of the main issues involved in employing people, you may want to become more acquainted with the following issues and how the law deals with them:

- terms of employment

- redundancy

- insolvency

- pregnancy

- suspension on medical grounds

- sick leave

- health and safety

- union membership

- itemised pay statements

- continuous employment

- time off for public duties

- unfair dismissal

- rights on ending employment

- union secret ballots

- limit on payment

- race discrimination

- sex discrimination

- equal pay

- disabled workers

- picketing

Although all of the above areas may not affect you, particularly in the early stages of development, if you do intend to employ staff then you should at least acquaint yourself with the areas.

Recruiting and motivating employees
Doing it yourself

You can do your own recruiting by advertising locally or in special; papers. Or you could write to colleges and schools for candidates.

Job centres and employment agencies

The Job Centre, the Job Club, or the local careers office are all in business to fit people to jobs. Job Centres or careers offices give their services for free, but an employment agency could cost you as much as 20% of the employees first years salary.

Training
Training is necessary to make sure that staff know why and how a job has to be done. It can also help make them

more efficient and help increase their productivity. Investing wisely in staff training pays off in the long run.

The personal approach

The better you treat your employees, the better they will treat you. If you are well mannered, punctual and committed they will be too. Show them that they are valued, encourage their interest in the business and ask them for suggestions. They will probably respond positively but don't be patronising.

Have confidence in your workforce and allow them to get on with the job. Checking everything they do creates resentment and not much else. All good managers are able to delegate. Good delegation is really what management is all about. You could also set targets and give bonuses. This way, you will encourage your employees to work harder. As a result you will increase productivity and waste less time. Payment-you must always pay wages on time and at competitive rates. Show appreciation-praise for a job well done is a real incentive. But try not to be over friendly. This is difficult when you are working one to one, but it might reduce your authority and it will be difficult to take a firm line if you ever need to.

7

Marketing

The next step in formulating our business plan is to look at sales, which in turn means looking at the market and considering the most appropriate form of market research. Sales are vital to any business. Whatever you produce, you must be able to sell. This is necessary in order to survive.

You must be satisfied that there is a demand for your proposed business and you must be able to determine how you can investigate the market in which you want to operate, how many potential clients there are in either the catchment area you operate in or the wider area. If you work in publishing for example then clearly the market for your product would be different for that of a baker or butcher or plumber. A lot of thought needs to be given to this area.

Market Research

The tool that is used to determine demand for a product is market research. Market research can be cheap and simple or highly complex depending on how you approach it and what you might want to find out.

Market research, or effective market research should be able to provide you with information as to what people want and also how much they want and what they will pay for it. Competition which might exist should also come to light.

You should not be put off by competition nor should you believe that because there appears to be no local supplier that what you produce will sell. No supplier may mean no demand and competition may mean established demand.

The concept behind all market research is simple-the practice is often not and unless you have a lot of money the costs may be prohibitive. A good example might be a supermarket.

A potential supermarket would want to know concrete facts in order to establish demand. For example, in terms of the percentage of the population, the average number of visits made to a supermarket each year. This they may well be able to establish from their own records if they are part of a chain.

Secondly they would want to know, what distance people are prepared to travel in order to visit a supermarket. This will vary a lot but they would be interested in establishing a national average.

With these two facts the supermarket can then establish the catchment area population for the proposed supermarket. Now they need to know something about the competition. How many supermarkets are there in the catchment zone which might have an effect on the proposed supermarket? This is easily established. However, more difficult to determine is the effect on your potential business. If we suppose that the supermarket decides that only 30% of the catchment area is exposed to competition and that they expect that 50% of that 30% would continue to use the supermarkets they presently use. This means an adjustment to predicted customer base.

However, competition comes from other shops not just supermarkets This is why calculations are based on average figures since this additional competition will be fairly standard throughout the country. A survey will be carried out in the locality to check that there are no special factors to consider-special factors which may cause adjustments to the predicted customer base either way.

The next question to be considered is; what is the average spend per visit per customer? Supermarkets will almost certainly be able to answer that one from existing records. From this data, they can predict gross sales and so the net operating profit. If this is not high enough to justify the expenditure, they might be reluctant to proceed with siting a supermarket.

The above is a simple model and does not take into account a number of complications but it does give an idea of how market research is carried out. There are two very important factors to be considered-average conditions in the industry and catchment area population, or a knowledge of that population. Although the example given covers selling to the general public the same principle applies when considering selling to other business.

It may be possible to determine industry averages by approaching trade associations. A visit to the bank is also very worthwhile as most high street banks keep statistics which they would be willing to make available. A further source of statistics might be a major supplier in an industry.

Somewhat easier is to determine the magnitude of the target market. Businesses generally fall into one or two categories: those where the customer comes to the business to place the order and those where the business goes to the customer to get the order.

In the first category, the size of your target market will be a percentage of the local population. The size of the population can be found by contacting the records office at your local authority. The percentage which applies to your proposed business will be far harder to determine. The classic method is simple-ask a large enough sample to provide an accurate picture. This is easier said than done. A great deal of research experience is necessary in order to be able to design a questionnaire which can elicit all the right information.

If you can afford it, you could consider employing a market research agency to assist you. If you cannot afford it then you should spend time considering exactly what you want to ask and what you are trying to establish. There are many other places which will hold the sort of information you might need. Your local training enterprise agency (TEC) or the trade association relevant to your business will be only too pleased to assist you.

Once you have established your target market, you might wish to consider exactly how you sell to that market. Easy if you have a shop in the middle of a busy shopping area, at least easier than if you produce books and have to cast your net far wider. It might be useful at this stage to look at marketing in a little more depth.

Marketing

You have carried out some form of research and now you are in a position where you wish to bring to peoples attention your product. Obviously different media are more suited to some businesses than others.

Marketing covers a whole range of activities designed to "identify, anticipate, and satisfy customer needs at a profit" (Chartered Institute of Marketing).

Three questions need to be looked at:

- When do customers want needs satisfied

- How do the customers want the need fulfilled

- How much are the customers prepared to pay for that fulfilment

Having found the answers to those questions we have to decide how best to communicate to the target market our ability to meet their needs at a price that they can afford- and communicate that ability to them at a price that we can afford.

There are various options that we can consider. However, some of these options are expensive and may well not be within our reach.

Advertising

Advertising takes various forms. It is exceedingly difficult, unless you have deep pockets, to try to deduce the real effectiveness of whichever form of advertising you decide to employ. For example, is it cost effective to spend £800 on a small advert in a tabloid for one day if that £800 could be spent on something longer lasting.

Advertising hoardings and posters are one way. These tend to cover not only billboards but also tubes trains and buses. Hoardings are seen repeatedly by a wide and ever changing audience in the locality of your choice. They are usually inexpensive.

Leaflets

Leaflets can be distributed on a door to door basis (either to other businesses or to individual residences) or they can be given to individuals in the street. However, leaflets can also be thrown away as many see them as junk mail. The result is that leaflets tend to have a low strike rate. Leaflets can also be delivered as inserts in magazines and newspapers. Magazines direct leaflets to specific audiences and newspapers to local areas. Both can prove expensive and again will be discarded more often than not.

A more effective use of leaflets is to have them available in places where the target market will see them. The classic case here is for businesses offering non residential facilities for holidaymakers. These can usually be found in hotels and guesthouses.

Another use of the leaflet is that of a poster in a newsagent or on other notice boards. This can be effective when being used to attract a defined group of the population who gather together in one place where leaflets cannot be made available. Universities or schools might be a good example.

Directories

Directories will fall into two categories-local and trade. Local directories such as yellow pages are well known mediums of advertising and they are reasonably priced, sometimes free. However, the effectiveness of such advertising depends on what you are doing and also where the ad is placed. Some businesses tend towards directories such as Thompsons because they have less advertisers and are cheaper.

Trade directories are different by their nature. They are unlikely to benefit new businesses as they can be expensive and are in some cases, nationally distributed.

This is of little use if your business is local, of more use if your product is distributed nationally. There are now a number of local area and regional directories, often produced by trade associations. Some are available as a book or on disc for use with computers. Those who subscribe to the disc system often receive monthly or quarterly updates.

Advertising in magazines

Magazines fall into three categories-general national, local or specialist. Magazines tend to be more expensive to advertise ion than newspapers but can be more effective. Magazines have a longer life expectancy than newspapers and are often passed on to other readers. Specialist magazines are read by specific people who may form part of your desired target audiences. It is worthwhile bearing in mind that most magazine are national.

Newspaper advertising

National newspapers can obviously reach a lot of people but also tend to be expensive. They are also of little value to those offering local services. Local newspaper advertising can be more effective and also cheaper. Free newspapers are cheaper but can be less effective as they also tend to be seen as junk mail.

Television advertising

It is highly unlikely that television advertising will be relevant in the early years of a business. To launch a television advertising campaign is very expensive indeed. Therefore, this medium will only be a consideration later on, if at all.

Radio advertising

This form of advertising would only be effective if there are sufficient numbers of listeners in the target market. However, in the right circumstances it can be useful and relatively inexpensive. Timing is very important in this medium as you need to target your slots at the most appropriate times and on the most appropriate programme for your intended target audience.

Using an advertising agent

Whether or not an advertising agency is employed will be a matter for the individual business concerned. This decision is down to cost. All businesses placing advertising should set an advertising budget. It could be that placing part of your budget with an agent proves far more cost effective than designing your own campaign. Agents are usually good at designing and placing adverts and can negotiate discounts with various media. It is certainly worthwhile consulting an agent in order to get an idea of what they can do for you, at the same time raising your own awareness of the direction you should be taking.

Direct mail

Direct mail falls into two categories: untargeted or blanket mailing or targeted. Targeted mail is usually far more effective as untargeted mail can be very expensive and also wasteful. Existing customers of a business are well defined and easily targeted. The secret with direct mail is to keep it short, simple and do it as often as is necessary.

Using sales representatives or agents

Whether or not you choose to use representatives or agents will depend on a number of factors. Where there are few sales required and the selling of a good is complex there may be the need for a representative. Where the product is simple and can be described in an advertisement or leaflet it is unlikely to be necessary to use a representative. There are two main types of representation, the representative or agent.

The representative is a paid member of staff who may or may not receive a bonus or commission based on results. All the representatives running costs will be borne by the business. An agent is a freelance who meets his or her own costs and is paid only on results.

The advantage of using the representative is that he or she uses their entire time devoted to your business and is under your total control.

The agent costs little to run. However, he or she is not totally dedicated to your business. If other products are easier to sell he may ignore yours altogether.

As you can see, there are a number of ways to reach your target audience, once that target audience has been defined. A lot of thought needs to be given to market research and marketing. All too often, they are the first areas to go through the window in search of savings or simply because you are too busy. However, well defined marketing can produce corresponding increase in profits and a clear strategy is an essential part of any business plan.

Pricing Your Product

A well thought out pricing plan is essential to the future prosperity of your business, and will also help you to make the most of your opportunities.

To develop the right pricing plan for your business, you need to start by working out what your costs are. You need to look at what your competitors are charging and try to estimate what your service or product is worth to your customers. By knowing what costs you are incurring, you will be able to work out what your "break even" point is. How much do you need to sell before your business covers all its costs, including your own (essential) drawings, but before it makes a profit. Unless you can identify what your break-even point is, you could operate at a loss, without realising until it is too late.

Your Costs

Costs can be divided into fixed (overheads) and variable (direct) costs. Fixed costs include your essential personal expenses, such as Mortgage, food etc, as well as rent, heating and lighting wages and interest charges. They tend to stay the same no matter how much you sell. Variable costs, however, increase or decrease according to your level of sales.

The most obvious cost here is the actual cost of materials required to manufacture the product but can include other things such as transport, postage or additional labour. The price you charge for your product has to cover all of the variable costs and contribute towards your overheads.

Outlined below is an example of a break-even point.

Fred Peters Car Wash Ltd	Cost per Annum
Personal Drawings	10,000
National Insurance	294
Tax	500
Stationary	100
Advertising	400
Telephone	320
Depreciation of Van (over 5 years)	1,000
Petrol	900
Servicing	300
Road Tax Fund	130
Insurance	320
Business Insurance	140
Materials	200
Depreciation of Equipment	200
Bank Loan £3,000 @ 12%	200
Bank Charges	100

Accountants Fees   300

TOTAL   £15,404

Fred's essential personal drawings to cover his family expenses is £10,000. He operates a small car wash. He expects to work for 46 weeks a year, allowing for holidays, sickness etc. He estimates that he will work 38 hours per week.

His annual output is therefore:

46 weeks a year Times 38 hours times 0.5 cars per hour = 874

His break even point is

$$\frac{15,404}{874}$$

= £17.62 per car

After researching the market in his area, Fred believes he can confidently charge £20 per car, which will give him a reasonable profit.

Competitors Prices

Unless your service or product is much better than others on the market, you would be unwise to charge a price which is too far above your competitors, as you will find sales very hard too achieve. On the other hand, a low price often implies low quality or low standards. Competing on price alone is a poor option. It is especially important for small businesses to differentiate themselves by other means, such as personal service, convenience or special skills. Customers rarely buy on price alone and it is worth remembering that you can more easily reduce your prices than put them up.

If, when you work out what your prices should be, they do not cover your costs-look again at how you might make your business viable. For example, could you reduce any of your variable costs, could you get supplies more cheaply, can you negotiate a discount or find an alternative supplier? On your fixed costs, could you trim any other expenditure?

Think again about what you are offering. Could it be improved and sold at a higher price? Can you sell different products for more money to increase your profits? Would sales increase if you put up your prices and spent the extra income on advertising and promotion?

Every cost incurred in running your business must be recovered either by what you charge for your time, or by the amount you charge for your products. Profits will be made only after all of your costs have been covered. But you may decide to use different prices in different situations. For example, a plumber offering a 24 hour service might decide to charge a premium rate for his services if he is called out during the night to deal with an emergency, a different rate for weekends and another rate for normal working hours.

Achieving a range of prices for the variety of skills offered, taking into account the time you would be likely to spend on each job and the convenience factor your customers can give you the flexibility to stay competitive, yet still provide a satisfactory income.

8

Financial Control

In this chapter, we will consider the importance of financial control within the process of business planning. In particular, we will look at profit and loss forecasting, cashflow forecasting, effective book-keeping, tax and insurance and raising capital for your business.

Profit and loss forecasting

A profit and loss forecast is a projection of what sales you think you will achieve, what costs you will incur in achieving those sales and what profit you will earn. There is a blank profit and loss forecast sheet in appendix to enable you to practice.

Having this information down on paper means that you will be able to refer to it, and adjust it as your business develops. Not all the headings will be relevant to you, so don't worry if you leave blank spaces.

There is an example of a profit and loss forecast overleaf which you can refer to.

Cashflow forecast

A cashflow forecast, as the name suggests, forecasts the changes in the cash which comes into and out of your bank account each month. For example, your customers may pay you after one month, whereas you might pay out for rent or insurance in advance. At the same time, you will have to pay for certain costs such as materials or wages and will need to budget for this.

Preparing a Cashflow Forecast

Remember that a cashflow forecast helps you to evaluate the timing of money coming into and going out of your business. In showing you the "movement" of money it takes full account of the fact that you may often not be paid immediately for work done and, correspondingly, that you may not have to pay immediately for goods and services you acquire. An important purpose of a cashflow forecast is to reveal the gap between your cash receipts and payments. It will show you whether or not, for example, you might need to borrow, and if so, when you are most likely to require additional funds. It is very common for businesses to need more cash as they grow because of the difference in timing of receipts and payments.

Other Terms

Working Capital
Working capital is the term often used to describe the short-term resources used by the business for everyday trading purposes. This consists of:

Debtors-these are customers you have sold to in credit, i.e., they owe you money.

Creditors-these are your suppliers who you have purchased from on credit, i.e., you owe them money.

Stock-this represents the value of materials you have purchased. They may be purchased for immediate resale or they may be in the process of being converted into a finished article.

Cash-this can either be the amount of physical cash you are holding or it may be money held in a current or bank deposit account.

All of the above have to be carefully controlled if your business is to prosper.

Over trading

A problem common to many small and growing businesses is what is described as "over trading". The more sales you make, the more money you will need to spend on funding material and debtors before you are paid for the sales. If your level of sales becomes too high and you do not have the necessary level of working capital to support it, you may simply run out of cash. This can be disastrous for your business and means that a full order book is not the only thing to strive for.

Even with a profitable business and a full order book, it is imperative to have enough cash available. Extra finance can help your cashflow and make it easier to avoid the pitfalls of over trading.

Collecting money on time

For every day a customer delays payments, your profit margin is eroded. You may have to pay interest charges on a loan or overdraft, when the money owed to you could be earning you interest instead.

Check your customers ability to pay

Before you offer customers credit, check that they can meet their liabilities. You may want to take up bank references.

Set out your terms of trading

Be specific about when you expect payment, for example, 30 days from the date of the invoice and make your customer aware in advance of work that you do.

Set up a system

Set up a system which enables you to issue invoices promptly and shows you when invoices become overdue.

Keep clear and accurate records

Inaccurate invoices or unclear records can be one of the main reasons for customers delaying payments. Make sure you send invoices punctually, to the right person at the right address.

Collect your payment on time

Establish a collections routine and stick to it. Keep records of all correspondence and conversations. Give priority to your larger accounts, but chase smaller amounts too. If regular chasing does not produce results consider stopping further supplies to the customer. If payment is not obtained, don't hesitate to ask a reputable debt collection agency or solicitor to collect the money for you.

Your Business activities will consist of selling goods and/or services. At the same time you will have to spend money on behalf of the business, on the purchase or rent of premises, raw materials, equipment, stationery etc. etc. in order to conduct business.

Remember that every business transaction generates a financial transaction, all of which must be recorded in books of account on an on-going basis. It is a fundamental management requirement that this be done on a regular basis, at a minimum once a week. Leave it much longer, and sooner or later an iron law of accounting will come into operation. You will have mislaid a financial record or simply forgotten to request one or issue one. When you do get around to up-dating the books, they won' balance. Unless you can discover the error before the end of the financial year your accountant will be faced with the task of reconciling "incomplete records", which he or she will enjoy because of the professional challenge but which costs you more money for more of his/her time.

What information must be kept?

As a minimum you must keep records of the following: -
i) All the invoices raised (or rendered) on behalf of the business, either when the goods are delivered or the services supplied, or shortly afterwards. An invoice is a

legal document and constitutes a formal demand for money. It must provide enough information to identify the business which sent it, who it was sent to, what it is for and whether VAT is payable.

ii) A list of your Sales invoices numbered sequentially.

iii) All Purchase invoices received, and listed i.e. those demands made on your business for the payment of money.

iv) Wages and salaries paid, and to whom; Income tax and NI contributions paid over to the Tax authorities.
v) All chequebook stubs, paying-in slips/books, counterfoils of petty cash vouchers, business bank account statements. Without these you cannot compile your books of account.

vi) A full record of VAT, whether paid by or paid to the business.

The advantages of a book-keeping system for your business

a) To provide accurate information sufficient to assess whether you are managing the business at a profit or a loss, or whether the business is solvent i.e. is there enough cash available in the business to pay all the outstanding liabilities on demand? The right information of the right kind at the right time is a vital management tool. Good management means making informed decisions of the right kind at the right time based on information that is true and therefore trustworthy.

b) To provide the information required for correct assessments of VAT and Income Tax, so as to avoid financial penalties (and possibly a suspect reputation) for incorrect and/or late payments. HM Customs & Excise keep records for seven years and the Inland Revenue keep them for three years, and so must you. Your accountant will need the best information in order to minimise your tax liabilities, unless of course you decide to submit a statement of income to your Inspector of Taxes without recourse to an accountant. In any event the Inspector will require a calculation of your Income from the business in the form of an Income and Expenditure Account for each trading year.

c) To monitor the behaviour of the business over time by reference to financial summaries "at a glance". You don't need to remember for example how many meals were served in your restaurant business say in this year compared with last year. The comparison that matters is the financial one with reference to the value of those transactions.

How to record the information you need

There are basically four methods of bookkeeping. Which one to choose will depend largely on the type and size of business you have established. Take advice from a business adviser or accountant if you are unsure as to which is the best one for your needs.

a) Proprietary systems.

These are best suited for sole traders in cash transaction types of business e.g. jobbing builders, market traders or some small shopkeepers. This type of business requires daily record keeping, often including till- rolls for the cash till and offers a simple method of control over finances.

A number of pre-printed stationery systems are available at business bookshops. Select one that allows you enough space to record all that needs recording. Worked examples are set out at the beginning of each book to show you how to keep cash records and the bank position, which can be calculated by following the instructions included. A list of business stationary systems publishers is found at the end of the book.

Cash businesses are more vulnerable than other types for the following reasons: -

i) It is far easier to lose or misplace paperwork. Therefore it is easier to lose control and lose money. Therefore it is more difficult to plan for the future.
ii) It is far more difficult to separate the cash that belongs in the business from the cash belonging to the proprietor.
iii) The Inland Revenue and HM Customs & Excise pay far closer attention to cash businesses because of the greater scope for "creative accounting" and tax evasion.

To minimise these risks, cash business-proprietors are strongly advised to pay their daily cash takings into the bank by using pre-printed paying-in books supplied by their bank. It is also vital to obtain receipts for purchases made from the takings and to keep them in an orderly fashion.

b) The Analysed Cash book System.

This is perhaps the most common method used by small businesses selling mostly on credit, with perhaps some cash sales. It relies on the Single Entry system of book-keeping, where each entry is, as the name implies, made once only, and all entries are made in one book, the Cash book. The analysed cash book is the "bible" of the business. It allows "at a glance" analysis because it is arranged on a columnar basis, showing how much has been received into the business, when and from where, how much of each receipt is attributable to VAT and therefore how much is the net amount belonging to the business. All this information is written up on one side of a pre-printed book, the left-hand page, showing all monies paid into the bank on behalf of the business. On the opposite, right-hand page are set out in separate columns details of what has been spent by the business, in other words, monies paid out of the bank, to whom and when.

This system is explained and illustrated in greater detail later in this chapter.

c) The Double Entry System

This method of recording accounts relies on ledgers, or separate books of account for each type of transaction. Far greater detail and control are possible using this system. As well as a cash account there is scope for setting up other ledgers such as the bought ledger for purchases, sales ledger, nominal (or business expense) ledger, salaries and so on.

It is much easier to monitor how much has been spent over a period of time on each type of transaction, simply by referring to the particular ledger or account, on each of which a running balance is struck. Every transaction is recorded in the major account called the Cash Account and also in the appropriate subsidiary ledger. In this way the Cash Account acts as a "Control" account for all the separate accounts of the business.

The most important feature of this system is the characterisation of all bookkeeping entries as either a "credit" ("he trusts" i.e." the business owes him") or "debit" ("he owes"). The sophistication of this method lies in the use of two entries for each transaction. For each credit entry in the Cash Account there must be a corresponding debit entry for the same amount in a different account. Likewise for each debit entry in the Cash Account there must be a corresponding credit entry in a different account. The key words are "equal and opposite". That way the greatest possible degree of control is obtained.

d) Computerised Accounting Systems

A wide variety of off-the-shelf packages are available, which rely on single or double entry methods. It may be tempting to invest in an accounts package at the outset, especially if you intend to use other computer packages in the business. It would be most unwise to start using such a package without understanding the principles that underlie them. Businesses have failed because of the familiar - "GIGO" - garbage in, garbage out. Money is the lifeblood of the business so don't turn it into garbage by neglecting an understanding of the what, why and how of bookkeeping.

Raising finance

It is probable that at some time you will need to borrow some money. Lenders have three basic considerations when looking at an application for a loan-the project, the people behind the project and the lending market currently existing.

There are a number of main options open to you for the financing of your business:

- Investment by an individual, either in the form of capital or a loan.

- Institutional investors

- Bank loans and overdrafts

- Grants, loans and assistance from government sources

- Payment from the Enterprise allowance

- Hire purchase or the leasing of plant

- Mortgage or rental of property

- Factoring of debts or invoices

- Loans against endowment policies

- Loans from suppliers in specialist industries

Any of the above categories of financing may be suitable for you and your business-more likely a combination of several. You should remember that every business decision has a financial implication and finding the right type of finance for your business could mean the difference between make or break.

It is highly advisable, if you need more detailed advice or assistance concerning finance, that you contact your local business advice centre. These centres are there to assist all potential or existing businesses and will provide someone who is expert in this particular field to advise you.

9

Your Business Plan

The following pages represent the basis for your business plan and the various sections relate to the sections of the book. If there are parts which you do not feel are relevant to your business, then you should ignore them.

You should construct your own business plan using the following as a guide. By referring to the book and also to the details of your own business you should be in a position to formulate your own plan which will be the complete document for your use, particularly for presentation to your bank manager or to other parties. Remember, it has been stressed throughout the book that an impressive business plan goes a long way towards developing your business and raising the necessary funds to go forward.

Your Business Plan

Name of business

_____

Address_____

_____

Telephone
Number_____

Sole Trader____   Partnership_____   Franchise___
Limited Company_____

Start up date_____
Type
Business_____

Planning ahead (see Chapter one)

My ultimate goal is

_____

_____

_____

_____

I expect to achieve the following over the next few years

Year
1_____

_____

Year
2_____

_____

Year
3_____

_____

Marketing

I have identified my market

as_____

_____

_____

_____

_____

_____

_____

_____

_____

_____

_____

My customers may be described
as_____

_____

_____

_____

_____

_____

_____

_____

_____

_____

_____

Product comparison table

_____

_____

     My Product   Competitor A
Competitor B

_____

_____

Price

_____

Quality

_____

Availability

_____

Customers

_____

Staff Skills

_____

Reputation

_____

Advertising

_____

Delivery

_____

Location

_____

Special Offers

_____

After Sales Service

_____

My product is special because

_____

_____

_____

_____

_____

_____

The main advantages of my product over my competitors are

_____

_____

_____

_____

_____

_____**Pricing**

Calculating your break even point

Personal Drawings

_____

_____

National Insurance

_____

_____

Tax

_____

_____

Stationary

_____

_____

Advertising

_____

_____

Telephone

_____

_____

Rent and Rates

_____

_____

Heating and Lighting

Vehicle Depreciation

_____

_____

Petrol

_____

_____

Servicing

_____

_____

Road Tax Fund

_____

_____

Insurance

_____

_____

Business Insurance

_____

_____

Bad Debts

_____

_____

Premises
My business will be located at

_____

_____

_____

_____

_____

Because

_____

_____

_____

_____

_____

Details of my lease/licence/rent/rate/next rent review

_____

_____

_____

_____

_____

_____

Details of key staff (if any

Name_____

_____

Position_____

_____

Address_____

_____Age_____

_____

Qualifications_____

_____

_____

Relevant work experience

_____

_____

_____

_____

_____

_____

Present
Income_____

_____

Repeat as necessary

I will need to buy in the following skills during the first two years

_____

_____

_____

_____

_____

I estimate the cost of employing people or buying any services I may need in the first two years

Number of people	Job Function	Monthly Cost

Annual cost

My personal Details
Name

Address

_____
_____
_____
_____
_____

Telephone
(home)_____
_____

Telephone
(work)_____
_____

Qualifications_____
_____
_____
_____
_____

Date of
Birth_____
_____

Business experience

_____

_____

_____

_____

_____

_____

Courses attended

_____

_____

_____

_____

_____

Book-keeping

I intend to keep the following records
(which will be kept up to date by myself/book-
keeper/accountant)

_____

_____

Other

Accountant

_____

_____

Address

_____

_____

Telephone_____

_____

Solicitor

Address

_____

_____

_____

_____

_____

_____

_____

Telephone_____

_____

VAT Number_____

Insurance
Arrangements_____

Raising finance

By reference to my profit and loss and cashflow forecast, I
need to borrow

Amount £

_____For

_____

_____

Period

_____

_____

I am investing £

_____

_____

_____

I can offer the following security

_____

_____

_____

_____

10

Raising Finance

Raising finance for your business can be difficult or relatively easy depending on the viability of your business and its ability to meet repayments and also the nature and type of assets that your business owns.

There are a number of alternatives when it comes to raising finance:

Investment of own funds

At the outset it is almost certain that you will have to invest some of your own time and money into your business. The investment will be financial, i.e. money which is an injection of your own funds into the business. If you are trading as a limited company this could take the form of a loan to the company or share capital. If you intend to operate as a sole trader or a partnership this will be owner's or partners capital.

The non-financial investment will take the form of assets that you already own, such as tools and equipment, or a vehicle. These will need to be valued for inclusion into the firms records and an accountant will almost certainly need to be employed to ensure that they are correctly valued and comply with relevant guidelines.

Financial gearing

This particular financial ratio is very important and measures the relationship between funds in the business and debt. For example if your business has £10,000 capital and you are seeking £15,000 of borrowed funds, then gearing is calculated by dividing one by the other, expresses in one of two ways:

Gearing percentage £15,000   divided £10,000 x 100 = 150%
Gearing ratio £15,000 divided by £10,000 = 1.5:1

The above demonstrates that for every £1 of capital there are debts of £1.50. Gearing of 100% is considered high gearing less than 100% considered low. If you are a small business looking for finance then a potential lender will be looking for gearing as close to 100% as possible. However, the type of finance you require, whether short or long term will also be a factor.

Short term finance

This type of finance is usually referred to as working capital finance. It is used to finance working capital and pay creditors and is then itself repaid following receipts of funds from debtors. The most common type of short-term finance is provided by banks in the form of an overdraft.

Trade credit
Obtaining credit from suppliers is also a type of short term finance. The terms of credit with a supplier will

vary according to the type of your business and the particular supplier.

Factoring

Factoring services have been used increasingly by small businesses in the last ten years or so, particularly those businesses who work for large companies or corporations who tend not to pay invoices for up to six months. Factoring enables you to bridge the gap between sending out an invoice and receiving payment. Factoring invoices has the advantage that you can receive immediate payment against an invoice, usually around 80% of face value. It has the disadvantage that there is a cost attached to it and it also has a stigma attached to it and can unsettle those with whom you do business with as it is perceived that you have cash flow problems.

Invoice discounting

This operates on broadly the same principle as factoring but with several differences:

- Control of the sales ledger is retained by you and it will be your responsibility to chase bad debtors, unlike factoring where the bank concerned (usually a bank) will undertake this function
- Because control is retained by you the existence of the arrangement wont be evident to customers

Long-term finance

If the finance is to be used to purchase any fixed asset then you must obtain long-term finance. It is good practice to raise the finance based on the life cycle of that fixed asset.

Business loans

Business loans can be raised from a number of sources. The usual source will be your bank if you already have a business account. Some loans are secured and some are unsecured. With all forms of business loans you need to know exactly what the terms are. Most loans are from £1,000-£1million and are repaid from 1 year to 20 years. You should consider the merits and demerits of fixed rate loans and variable loans. This will be influenced by the economic climate currently prevailing.

The Small Firms Loan Guarantee Scheme

This scheme (SFLGS) is a joint scheme operated by the Small Business Service (SBS) and a consortium of lenders including high street banks. It is available to small businesses that have a viable business plan but cannot get a conventional business loan. Under the scheme the government provides a guarantee to the funder against default by the borrower, for 70% of the loan. For business that have been trading for longer than two years this increases to 85%. The minimum loan (at time of writing) is £5,000 the maximum £100,000 and for firms that have been trading for at least two years the amount is £250,000.

Hire purchase and leasing
Hire purchase is a very flexible and relatively easy to obtain form of funding, often used to purchase assets.

Leasing is a flexible form of funding. A lease is negotiated with the lessor. Assets that are leased can vary from office furniture to heavy machinery to vehicles. Leasing is distinguished from hiring. Hiring requires the hirer to select an item which is already in stock whilst with leasing an item can be chosen from any manufacturer or supplier. The subsequent lease agreement will be tailor made for the asset involved. There are three types of lease:

- Finance lease
- Operating lease
- Contract hire

Finance leases

With a finance lease the lessor pays for the asset and becomes the owner. The lessee then pays a hire charge which covers the capital cost of the asset and also interest and service charges. The lessee is responsible for all subsequent maintenance and insurance.

Operating lease

This type of lease is, in the main, undertaken by the manufacturer of products that tend to be highly specialised or technical. The lease will usually provide that the lessor is responsible for all future servicing, maintenance and updating of equipment.

Contract hire

This is similar to an operating lease. One of the most common uses of contract hire is to finance a fleet of motor vehicles. In the case of contract hire, the lessor will take responsibility for all future maintenance and costs, the lessee has only to find fuel costs.

Soft loans

These sorts of loans are available usually on more generous terms and are made through local Enterprise Agencies and are available when conventional funding is not.

There are other forms of finance available which would not really be relevant to small business start ups, such as equity finance, where a proportion of the business is given up for finance and venture capital, which is only really for larger investments.

11

Looking at Franchises

A franchise is a business relationship between the franchisor who has a tried and tested business concept and the franchisee who will purchase the right to operate this business. A Franchise will involve a capital investment and payment of ongoing royalties or management fees based on sales-turnover or as a mark up on goods supplied for resale by the franchisor.

Advantages and disadvantages of a franchise

The main advantage of buying a franchise is that you will be buying a tried and tested business idea. Although usually not cheaper than starting your own business you are cutting out all the steps to achieving brand recognition. There are lots of benefits to buying a franchise, the main ones being:

- You will be purchasing a business concept that has been tried and tested in the marketplace
- Lower risks in initial set-up
- Business premises will all comply with a blueprint, which satisfies all regulations
- Publicity and ongoing marketing will be supplied by the franchisor as will training and education in the business field

- Networking opportunities will be available with other franchisors
- You will be operating in a defined geographical area.

In addition to the above, gaining funding to start a franchise is a good deal easier (depending on the franchise) than a start up business. In some circumstances, the franchisor may be able to offer funding for the franchise start up.

The disadvantages

Like most things in life, there are down sides. Once a franchise is purchased, it can be difficult to dispose of it as there are often terms imposed as to resale. Disputes can arise as to the royalty or management fee and there is also the possibility that the franchisor may fail leaving you with a business that may not be viable in isolation.

Different types of franchise

There are franchising opportunities available for all sorts of businesses. In order to assess whether a business is suitable for franchise there are a number of factor which you need to consider:

- the main one-the original business concept must have been tried and tested and proven to be a success.
- The franchise must have a distinct brand image and tried and tested methods

- Operation of the franchise must be profitable and provide the franchisor with a limit

If you look in some popular papers, such as Daltons Weekly, you can see a whole proliferation of business that are for sale as so-called franchises. It is, or should be immediately obvious, that such businesses are highly suspect. It is necessary to look at the characteristics of a business for sale to gauge whether or not it is suitable for franchise. These characteristics will include:

- Products that have a very short life span in the market
- Businesses with minimal profitability
- Business with repeat business based on loyalty to an individual rather than a product or service
- Businesses that are specific to one geographical area.

There are three types of franchise:

- Job franchise-where effectively you are purchasing a job for yourself. These franchises will be one-person businesses and will require you to invest up to £20,000. Examples range from carpet cleaning to vehicle repair.
- Business franchise. Somewhat more complex as these involve the purchase of a complete business with staff. These types of franchise can cost up to £100,000. Such franchises will include fast food outlets and print shops.

- Investment franchises. These are at the top end and usually include hotels and restaurants and a substantial investment will be required, often up to £1 million.

Beware when entering into a franchise. As mentioned there are many 'scams' out there. It is highly advisable to go to one of the franchising conferences, held in the main cities, in order to gain a better idea of what the franchising world is all about.

12

Buying an Existing Business

There are many businesses available for sale in all areas of the market and this is, sadly, an area where many people end up losing out, usually to people or concerns that are trying to offload a business that is failing.

Inspecting a business for sale

If you have identified a business that interest you, it will be necessary to make a number of visits to that business and to carry out a number of 'due diligence' checks. In addition to appraising the business from the standpoint of its operations, such as the flow of customers, attitude of the staff, premises and stock, it is essential that you have a handle on the valuation of the business. Many times business are overvalued and overstate their turnover. It is vital to involve professionals, such as lawyers and accountants at the outset. This may cost but is nothing compared to the cost to you if you buy a business and realise that it is failing.

There will be a number of elements involved in forming the price of a business, such as building and stock. It will be essential to ensure that a correct appraisal is carried out. Are the assets as valuable as they are said to be, i.e. their book value? Is the total turnover accurately stated and is it a realistic appraisal of ongoing year on year turnover. Where are the risks?

You will also need to examine the following:

- Trade debtors
- Trade creditors
- Other creditors
- Any agreements such as hire purchase and leases, including leases on buildings
- Bank loans

Basically you will need to ensure that you are not purchasing a risk and that all agreements in place will apply to you when you purchase a business.

Goodwill

There is usually an amount involved for 'goodwill' in a business. This will be the payment for having built up the business and their brand name and their commercial reputation.

Extreme care should be taken in this area. The owner will argue that they have spent years building up the business. The counter argument will be that benefits have been taken out of the businesses over the years which have been produced by the development of goodwill. A professional appraisal of this area is definitely needed.

The process of purchasing a business

When you have been through the process of due diligence, it will be necessary to employ the services of a lawyer who specialises in the sale of commercial properties. This person will draw up a suitable contract of sale, compile a schedule of assets and liabilities that are to be included in the sale and the agreed valuation, search companies house for details of all existing directors and shareholders and other information and complete the necessary forms to register the transfer.

Although this chapter has been brief, the main message is BEWARE when buying a business and carry out a thorough investigation of what you are buying. Look out for any cover-ups and any likely future risks and make sure, before you enter into the purchase that you are totally committed.

Useful Addresses

Advertising Association
Abford House
15 Wilton Road
London SW1 1NJ
020 7828 2771
www.adasocc.org

Advisory Conciliation and
Arbitration Service (ACAS)
Clifton House
83-117 Euston Road
London NW1 2RB
Tel 0207 369 5100
www.acas.org.uk

British Chambers of Commerce
Manning House
22 Carlisle Place
London SW1P 1JA
Tel 0207 565 2000
www.britishchambers.org

Association of Chartered Certified Accountants
29 Lincolns Inn Field
London
WC2A 3EE
020 7242 6855
www.acca.org.uk

Association of Independent
Business

38 Bow Lane
London EC4M 9AY
Tel 0207 329 0219

BNR Business Names Registration
Somerset House
Temple Street
Birmingham B2 5DN
Tel 0207 643 0227

British Franchising Association, Franchise Chamber
Thames View
Newtown Road
Henley on Thames
Oxon RG9 1HG, Tel 01709 578049
www.british-franchise.org.uk

British Overseas Trade Board
1-3 Victoria Street
London SW1E 6RB
Tel 0207 215 5000
British Technology Group
101 Newington Causeway
London SE1 6BU
Tel 0207 403 6666

British Venture Capital Association
Essex House
12-13 Essex Street
London WC2R 3AA
020 7240 3846
www.bvca.co.uk

Business in the Community
8 Stratton Street
Mayfair
London W1X 6AH
Tel 0207 629 1600

Business Links
See local phone books or
Small firms and business links
Division

Business Names Registration plc
Somerset House
Temple Street
Birmingham
B2 5DN
0121 643 0227

Department of Trade and Industry
Level 2
St Marys House
Sheffield S1 4PQ
Tel 0114 259 7507

The Chartered Institute of
Patent Agents
Staple Inn Buildings
High Holborn
London WC1V 7PZ
Tel 0207 405 9450

Chartered Institute of Marketing
Moor Hall
Cookham
Maidenhead
Berkshire
SL6 9QH
01628 427 500
www.cim.co.uk

Companies Registration Office
Companies House
Crown Way
Cardiff
CF4 3UZ
Tel 01222 388588

Confederation of British
Industry (CBI)
Centrepoint
103 New Oxford Street
London WC1A 1DU
Tel 0207 379 7400
www.cbi.org.uk

Department of Social Security
Richmond House
79 Whitehall
London SW1A 2NS
Tel 0207 210 5983
Freephone 0800 666 555

Department of Trade and Industry
1-3 Victoria Street

London SW1E 6RB
Tel 0207 215 5000
www.dti.gov.uk

Department for Education and Employment
Moorfoot
Sheffield S1 4PQ
Tel 0114 275 3275

Export Market Information Centre
Kingsgate House
66-74 Victoria Street
London SW1E 6SW
020 7215 5444
www.tradepartners.gov.uk

Forum for Private Business
Ruskin Chambers
Drury Lane
Knutsford
Cheshire WA16 6HA
Tel 01565 634467

Grants and Funding Information
www.grantsnet.co.uk
www.j4b.co.uk

Health and Safety Executive
Chancel House
Neasdon Lane
London NW10 2UD
Tel 0208 459 8855

Institute of Trade Mark Agents
Canterbury House
2-6 Sydenham Road
Croydon
CRO 9XE
International Association of
Bookkeepers
Burford House
44 London Road
Sevenoaks
Kent TN13 1AS
Tel 01732 458080

National Federation of Enterprise Agencies
Trinity gardens
9-11 Bromham Road
Bedford
MK40 2UQ
01243 354 055
www.nfea.com

National Federation of
Small Businesses
32 Orchard Road
Lytham St Annes
Lancashire FY8 1NY
Tel 01253 720911

Scottish Enterprise
120 Bothwell Street
Glasgow G2 7JP
Tel 0141 248 2700

Small Business Service
www.businessadviceonline.org

Small Firms Loan Guarantee Scheme
0845 001 0032
www.dti.gov.uk/sflg/
The Patent Office
0645 500505
E mail enquiries enquiries@patent.gov.uk

Welsh Development Agency (WDA)
Pearl House
Greyfriars Rd
Cardiff CF1 3XX

English Enquiry 0345 775577
Welsh Enquiry 0345 775566

Index